This is a gift from the:

Danville Library
Foundation

CREEPY CREATURES

BIGTOOT

Big Buddy Books
An Imprint of Abdo Publishing
abdopublishing.com

Sarah Tieck

abdopublishing.com

Published by Abdo Publishing, a division of ABDO, PO Box 398166, Minneapolis, Minnesota 55439.
Copyright © 2016 by Abdo Consulting Group, Inc. International copyrights reserved in all countries. No part
of this book may be reproduced in any form without written permission from the publisher. Big Buddy Books™
is a trademark and logo of Abdo Publishing.

Printed in the United States of America, North Mankato, Minnesota.
042015
092015

Cover Photo: Blend RF/Glow Images.
Interior Photos: ASSOCIATED PRESS (pp. 7, 13, 17, 24); Deposit Photos (p. 22); Eighth Street Studio (p. 7);
    ©iStockphoto.com (pp. 5, 9, 17, 19, 21, 30); © Photos 12/Alamy (p. 23); © Ronald Grant Archive/Alamy (p. 22);
    Shutterstock.com (pp. 21, 25, 29); Standard-Examiner, Nick Short/AP Images (p. 27); © Steppenwolf/Alamy
    (p. 11); Angel Wynn/Native Stock (p. 15).

Coordinating Series Editor: Rochelle Baltzer
Contributing Editors: Tamara L. Britton, Bridget O'Brien, Marcia Zappa
Graphic Design: Jenny Christensen

Library of Congress Cataloging-in-Publication Data

Tieck, Sarah, 1976- author.
  Bigfoot / Sarah Tieck.
    pages cm. -- (Creepy creatures)
  ISBN 978-1-62403-764-1
1. Sasquatch--Juvenile literature. I. Title.
  QL89.2.S2T54 2016
  001.944--dc23
                        2015002630

Contents

Creepy Bigfoot

   People love to tell spooky stories, especially about creepy creatures such as Bigfoot. They speak of giant footprints in the forest. They share pictures and videos of a large, hairy being. And, some report a terrible smell!

   Bigfoot has appeared in books, stories, plays, television shows, and movies. But is this creature real, or the stuff of **legend**? Let's find out more about Bigfoot, and you can decide for yourself!

Pictures of Bigfoot are often unclear.

Did you know?

Bigfoot goes by different names around the world. These include Sasquatch, Yeti, and Abominable Snowman.

5

Scary Stories

   Stories describe Bigfoot creatures as being between 6 and 15 feet (2 and 5 m) tall. Depending on where they live, these beasts have dark or light fur. Their faces resemble human faces.

   People say Bigfoot creatures take large steps with bent knees and swinging arms. Though they may be quiet, sometimes Bigfoot creatures make high-pitched howls or cries.

People hold meetings to share information about Bigfoot.

Some people believe Bigfoot's bad smell helps protect it and warn others, like a skunk's smell.

Stories tell of large footprints found in dirt and snow in natural areas, such as forests. Some believe they are from Bigfoot. These creatures eat a range of foods from plants to animals. Their hairy bodies help them survive in very cold weather.

One area Bigfoot creatures are believed to live in is the mountains of California, Oregon, and Washington.

Living History

In 1811, British explorer David Thompson found a very large footprint in Canada. It was a total of 8 inches (20 cm) wide and 14 inches (36 cm) long. It included four toes that were 3 to 4 inches (8 to 10 cm) long. Each toe had a claw. Thompson's finding is considered the first **evidence** of Bigfoot.

Thompson wrote about his experiences exploring parts of the United States and Canada (*right*) in a book. In it, he describes finding the large footprint and choosing not to follow whatever made it.

Many stories of Bigfoot sightings have been told over the years. In 1967, Roger Patterson and Robert Gimlin filmed a video near Bluff Creek, California. It showed a large creature that looked like Bigfoot. But, many believe it was a trick.

Today, people continue searching for Bigfoot. They have collected **evidence**. However, much of it is still in question. Some has been proven false.

Gimlin (*left*) and Patterson (*right*) made casts of some Bigfoot footprints.

Around the World

There are stories of Bigfoot creatures in many **cultures**. In western Canada and the northwestern United States, people talk of Sasquatch, or "wild men." Native Americans have Sasquatch **legends**, too. Some Pacific Coast tribes carve or paint Sasquatch on masks or **totem poles**.

On the Atlantic Coast, the Delaware Native Americans tell of a spirit called Living Solid Face. It is represented by a mask that is half red and half black. Recently, some people have connected the spirit with Bigfoot creatures.

The Delaware believe Living Solid Face guards all animals.

In Asia, people have talked about the Abominable Snowman since 326 BC! This hairy, white creature is also called the Yeti. It has big teeth. Its arms stretch to its knees.

In 1951, Eric Shipton took pictures of large footprints in south Asia's Himalayas. Many groups have taken special trips to this mountain range to look for Yetis. But, no one has found a body or bones to prove Yetis are real.

Yetis are said to have been seen on Mount Everest, which is in the Himalayas.

Shipton's footprint photos were sold. So far, footprints, sightings, photos, and videos are the only signs of Bigfoot creatures.

Good or Evil?

People fear Bigfoot creatures. In stories, they are wild creatures that are hungry for flesh and blood. They may attack people or villages.

A Bigfoot's size alone is enough to be scary. Some are said to be up to 15 feet (5 m) tall. That is more than twice the height of most adult men. A Bigfoot's feet may measure up to 16 inches (41 cm) long and 7 inches (18 cm) wide!

It is not known if Bigfoot creatures live alone or with others.

In some stories, people fear Bigfoot creatures because they seem strong and **unpredictable**. But then, they discover a Bigfoot is actually just lonely and afraid. The monster may be able to make friends and help others.

Many people think Bigfoot legends are fun! Statues and signs showing the creatures are common in areas where they are believed to live.

The Bumble

In 1964, the Bumble appeared in the movie *Rudolph the Red-Nosed Reindeer*. It was also called the Abominable Snow Monster of the North.

Harry

In 1987, *Harry and the Hendersons* came out. In this movie, Harry is a friendly Bigfoot-type creature who becomes part of a family.

Bigfoot in Pop Culture

Marshmallow

In the 2013 movie *Frozen*, this snow beast guards Queen Elsa and her ice palace. He is very strong and scary. But unlike other Bigfoot creatures, he is made from snow, ice, and magic.

Expedition Everest

This Disney World roller coaster takes riders on a speeding train. Riders race through the icy Himalayas and try to escape the Yeti!

Messin' with Sasquatch

Starting in 2006, Jack Link's Beef Jerky made funny **advertisements**. A Sasquatch was the star of these ads.

Fact or Fiction?

Scientists cannot prove Bigfoot creatures are real. Still, many people have footprints, photos, or videos. They also collect hair, bones, and other objects that may provide proof. Scientists often find these are from other animals, such as bears or even humans.

Today, people continue to disagree in spite of centuries of stories. No one knows for sure if Bigfoot exists. But each passing year brings more possible **evidence** to consider.

Evidence people have collected includes objects that resemble fossils (*below*). A scientist found this was not a Bigfoot skull, but just an unusual rock. It did not prove Bigfoot creatures exist.

What Do You Think?

So, what do you think about Bigfoot? Does it still send a chill up your spine? It can be fun to watch spooky Bigfoot movies or to dress as Bigfoot on Halloween.

It is also interesting to learn about Bigfoot. Knowing what is true and what is made up is powerful. Whether you read **fiction** about Bigfoot or search for real-life **evidence**, you are in for an exciting journey.

People who go into the wild looking for Bigfoot and other legendary creatures are called cryptozoologists (krihp-tuh-zoh-AH-luh-jihsts).

Let's Talk

What examples of Bigfoot stories can you think of?

What would you do if you spotted Bigfoot and took a video of it?

How do you think it would feel to be Bigfoot?

If you were to write a story about Bigfoot, where would you set it? How would you have your Bigfoot interact with people?

Imagine that you are a scientist wanting to find Bigfoot. Where would you go to look? What **evidence** would you want to find?

Glossary

advertisement (ad-vuhr-TEYZE-muhnt) a short message in print or on television or radio that helps sell a product.

culture (KUHL-chuhr) the arts, beliefs, and ways of life of a group of people.

evidence facts that prove something is true.

fiction stories that are not real.

legend an old story that many believe, but cannot be proven true.

totem pole a Native American pole carved and painted with symbols that tell legends, history, and family stories.

unpredictable not able to be seen or known in advance.

Websites

To learn more about Creepy Creatures, visit **booklinks.abdopublishing.com**. These links are routinely monitored and updated to provide the most current information available.

Index